THE LIBRARY OF INTERIOR DETAIL

MAISON

THE LIBRARY OF INTERIOR DETAIL

MAISON

*French
Country Style*

ELIZABETH HILLIARD

PHOTOGRAPHS BY JOHN MILLER

BULFINCH PRESS
LITTLE, BROWN AND COMPANY
BOSTON • NEW YORK • TORONTO • LONDON

First North American Edition
First printed in Great Britain in 1994 by Pavilion Books Limited

ISBN 0-8212-2072-1
Library of Congress Catalog Card Number 93-80209

Bulfinch Press is an imprint and trademark of
Little, Brown and Company (Inc.)
Published simultaneously in Canada by
Little, Brown & Company (Canada) Limited

PRINTED IN ITALY

CONTENTS

A charming Christmas wreath of dried grasses, hung on the door of a house in the Camargue to signify joyful seasonal greetings. It is suspended by a sash of traditional Provençal fabric from Souleiado.

INTRODUCTION

WHEN ONE THINKS OF FRENCH COUNTRY STYLE, AN IMAGE IMMEDIATELY SPRINGS TO mind. The scene is set in the dappled shade of a plane tree near the windows of a low stone house, shutters closed against the baking heat. Brilliant, hot sunshine has already begun to bleach last year's fresh coats of rich pink paint on the outside walls and the blue of the plank shutters. A wooden table is covered with a brightly patterned cloth and has been laid for a meal, with plain white china, thick glass tumblers, simple stainless steel cutlery, and a thick, pressed linen napkin beside each place. Sounds of laughter and food preparation waft out from a door in the building beyond. You enter and find yourself in a cavernous kitchen.

The large, French country kitchen is as much a place to meet and gossip as to cook and eat – providing the chat does not distract from the serious business of cooking. The sound of corks popping from bottles of rosé and the mouthwatering scents of cooking garlic, rosemary and the classic Provençal ratatouille accompany you as you make your way around the room. You notice the row of copper pans hanging on the wall – gleaming russet-gold vessels in a dozen sizes, each with its own special purpose.

You move on to admire shelves weighed down with local faience and marbled pottery, the magnificent wide cooker, beneath the canopy of the kitchen's vast fireplace,

The collection of eggy objects on these kitchen shelves was inspired by the fine metal wirework of the baskets on the top shelf, which date from around 1900.

bearing bubbling and steaming pans, and the fat bunches of herbs hanging to dry from the ceiling. People start to make their way outside and you follow them; the feasting is about to begin ...

You are in Provence in summer, a place which has captured our collective imagination as being the epitome of the French countryside. The landscape and architecture of France vary hugely, from the half-timbered German-looking homes of Alsace to the stone-roofed houses set in the woods and hills of the Dordogne, but nowhere seems more French than Provence.

Food and the kitchen are at the heart of French country style, whatever the region. Food is an art form here, and the contemplation and consumption of it a national pastime. Even if the kitchen is small, more likely in the cities than in a château or converted farmhouse, it is always beautiful. Equipment is kept in peak condition. Rather than being hidden behind the cupboard doors of expensive kitchen units, it is often proudly displayed on open shelves, along with the pottery and china, ever ready to leap into action.

French kitchen equipment is among the best in the world (even if the French have rejected the idea of a kettle for boiling water), from the Le Creuset casseroles found in every English 'farmhouse' kitchen, to the gargantuan stainless-steel pans used by professional chefs everywhere. In the production of copperware, stainless-steel ware and pottery, the French are unrivalled. Swiss copper pans may be of equal quality, but they are made in only a fraction of the range of sizes available from France. When a recipe calls for a particular cooking utensil, most of us 'make do' with whatever comes to hand, whereas the French will use the exact type and size of pan specified.

The Provençal kitchen which fulfils our idea of the epitome of French country style is a spacious room – or it would be were it empty of furniture. For in addition to the equipment and furniture you would expect to find in a kitchen, including of course a large solid table, it has some special items such as the *panetière*. Known locally in Provence as a *panière*, this is a wall cupboard for storing freshly-baked bread. It is also an opportunity for the Provençal cabinetmaker to show off his skill at joinery, turning and carving, and generally to enjoy himself.

A *panetière* looks like a miniature pipe organ without a keyboard, on account of the many turned bars around the sides. The roof of the cupboard is crowned at the corners with top-knots known as *bobèches* or *chandelles*, sometimes sporting a whole regiment of these flourishes. The bottom has the four feet upon which all *panetières* once stood before someone thought of hanging theirs on a wall. The central door and horizontal panels above and below are vehicles for flamboyant carving. This might consist of simple curling lines, flower or heart shapes, or of elaborate urns, baskets, wheatsheafs, eglantine flowers and trailing vine leaves or myrtle.

Another important piece of furniture in the country kitchen and dining room is the *armoire*, a huge storage cupboard which was traditionally part of a bride's dowry. On these too craftsmen carved exuberant decoration which was often related to the event of a girl's marriage – sheaves of wheat or bunches of grapes, for example, refer- ring to her hoped-for fertility. An *armoire* has two doors closing onto a narrow central upright. Traditionally, each door has three panels with curving edges, and between these and the inside edge of each door, the finest examples have *ferrures*. These are narrow, lacy strips of iron or steel which are highly decorative, whilst protecting the doors from the effects of greasy fingers opening and closing them. Country furniture was inevitably made from wood which is plentiful locally, and in Provence that tradi- tionally meant walnut.

Observers have noticed that the prevailing culture of fine food and wine, bars and

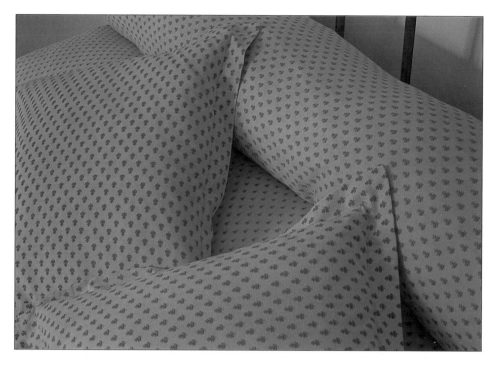

A traditional Provençal print has been used here to cover a modern brass bed, its pillows and bolster. Tiny repeated prints comparable to these were especially popular in France in the 1800s. Napoleon is reputed to have bought lengths of the fabric for Josephine and the ladies of the court.

restaurants, and entertaining and eating away from home, has had a highly significant effect on the interior of French homes. With the emphasis on going out, the home has become hardly more than a base in which to sleep and keep your clothes.

In addition, the French attitude differs from that of other countries in that there is not the same mania for throwing out the furnishings and decorations of a few years ago in favour of a new look, be it ultra modern or, more likely in recent decades, flowers and frills or Victorian style. On the contrary, if furnishings still serve a practical purpose and are pleasing to the eye, why change them for change's sake? For example, fabrics such as Provençal prints and toile de Jouy are both immensely popular, even though, perhaps because, they each have a history going back centuries.

Toile is an instantly recognizable fabric which traditionally shows pastoral scenes from mythology and the classics (and, occasionally, historic events such as the first hot air balloon ascent and the American War of Independence) in a single colour on white or cream. Set up in 1770 in Jouy-en-Josas near Versailles, the first factory used copperplate printing to create the images on imported Indian calico. The fabrics were a success and in 1806 the founders (who were, ironically, German) set up their own cotton mill. Provençal prints are derived from *indiennes*, colourful Indian textiles imported into Marseilles in the seventeenth century. French versions were first manufactured there in 1656 and they were also made in Avignon.

The widespread popularity of these prints declined in the nineteenth century, and it looked as though the industry and tradition of these bright, printed floral and geometric fabrics, with their distinctive strong colours and repeating designs, might disappear completely.

However, during the second half of the twentieth century, traditional Provençal fabrics have undergone a renaissance, mainly thanks to one man. Charles Deméry took over a fabric printing company in 1938 and rescued an astonishing collection of 40,000 wooden printing blocks. These formed the basis of the designs on fabrics sold by the company Souleiado ever since. After the war years this company upgraded production, converting to synthetic dyes and large-scale roller printing methods, and the popularity of the fabrics rose once again. Today the name Souleiado is world-famous, and has become synonymous with Provençal patterns and colours. Such popularity can only have helped the few other small companies that also produce traditional Provençal prints. Souleiado fabrics, meanwhile, are available in many countries outside France, and the company also produces a large catalogue of its designs which is available by mail order (see page *80* for details).

Another consideration affecting the look of French homes is the fact that among owners of old homes in particular, DIY has never been perceived as a jolly weekend activity involving the whole family, as it is elsewhere. If you need something done, you hire a professional who knows what he or she is about and will do a job that will last.

This beautiful iron table was found in the cellar when the current owners moved into their 1810 house near Moulins, right in the heart of France. The chair is early twentieth century; the cloth is a magnificent 'table carpet', a thickly woven fabric, with the vibrant colours and flamboyant design of the style of Napoleon III.

In recent decades there has been some increased interest in interior decoration in France. The President's palace, L'Elysée, is now regularly redecorated to create a showcase for the best of French decoration and design. But in the meantime, the average French home has escaped the frills and fuss of some styles of decoration. The result is a fresh, simple look based on the lines of the building itself and the function of the objects within, which themselves have a direct, graphic quality which makes them eminently desirable.

Since the beginning of the twentieth century, a large shift in population has taken place in France, and this too has had an effect on French interiors. In 1900 as much as half the population lived in the country. Today that number has dropped to well below ten per cent. This migration to the cities has resulted in large numbers of agricultural buildings and country houses coming onto the market. The new owners are city people or foreigners acquiring a holiday home; they are people such as artists and craftsmen who do not need to be in the city for their work; they are businesspeople who can do most of their work from home with the aid of computers, telecommunications and other modern technology; or they are wealthy people 'getting away from the smog', leaving behind the dirt and stress of their former urban existence. Whoever they are, they are not the traditional peasant in blue cotton overalls, his *bleu de travail*, with his wife swathed in black.

The newcomers have brought with them a dash of elegance and sophistication which blends well with their hearty admiration for all things French and for the ways of the countryside into which they have moved. The wealthier locals have themselves become more sophisticated, meanwhile, adopting the best of modern ways. One of the houses photographed for this book is a traditional *mas* (farmhouse) in the Camargue – complete with fax machine.

Light shining through the pattern in a crocheted throw draped over an elegant banquette.

This new French style, a sort of *style haut paysan*, exists alongside a country style that derives from France's proud history of centuries of interior decoration in the grand manner. The impetus and money for such enterprise came from royalty and the top echelons of noble and wealthy society, and examples can be seen today in the many châteaux open to the public. While the fruits of this tradition, its furniture and objets, are sought after across the world, at home in France it continues, albeit generally on a more modest scale.

In the mid-1970s, I visited a home with echoes of this tradition, whose quietly opulent elegance would have been alarming had it not been so comfortable and seductive. The house, in a small town in the Loire valley, was stone-built and of a comfortable size rather than enormous, with four bedrooms. Its proportions were not imposing, but its decoration seemed to me to be as grand, in parts, as any stately home I had ever visited as a tourist.

The most fascinating room was the study or library, in which the family sat when they wished to be cosy. Never had I seen so much rich, vibrant pattern in one room. The sofas and chairs were upright and tapering, quite unlike the large, squashily embracing sofas found in an English country house. They were all covered with the same bold fabric of traditional design, showing thick ropes of intertwined rich red and pink flowers and green foliage against a white background.

But the thing that bowled you over was the fact that the *walls* were covered with this fabric too. How was it done? Enquiries revealed that the fabric was nailed to thin battens of wood which were in turn fixed to the walls. But I never saw a single tell-tale nail or screw, the fabric was as smooth as ice, without a single gather or tuck, and all the lines of the pattern were straight. It was a marvel of decorating at which I gazed in awe. My hosts were amused by this strange child's interest.

One wall of this room was occupied by a huge bookcase, the type of large piece of furniture which dominates so many French country living rooms. Its upper doors were glazed so that one could see the collection housed within. This included some leather-bound books with gold lettering on their spines. Far more interesting, however, were the objects lying in front of the books – arranged there, one might say, had their 'arrangement' not appeared so entirely artless, in the same way that the clothes and appearance of a French man or woman can seem so effortlessly elegant. No other country has such a reputation for this gift.

In the bookcase, ivory opera glasses, tiny kid gloves, elaborate silver and enamel boxes, a fountain pen, small bronze animals, an exquisite linen and lace handkerchief embroidered with the letter 'E', miniature portrait paintings of forebears, babies' teething rings and christening mugs … so many small treasures of great age and beauty were here massed together so nonchalantly.

This net curtain is of a type known as 'château curtains', and is made from a hand-embroidered fine cotton voile. The draped curtain is actually a nineteenth-century linen sheet with a seam along the middle, indicating that it was domestically made on a small loom.

Other rooms in a French country house can seem surprisingly spartan by contrast with the warmth and elegance of living rooms and bedrooms. Bathrooms are often purely utilitarian, unfitted and plain white, decorated from floor to ceiling with gleaming

*One curving end of a traditional nineteenth-century French 'lit bateau', literally
'boat bed'. The quilt was found in a Lyon fleamarket.*

white tiles, and without any apparent concession to comfort. Baths and basins are large and heavy, massive reminders of a previous age.

One of the things which surprised me on my first visit to France was a detail which in retrospect seems small and rather charming. There were no chests of drawers. Not in my bedroom; nor, apparently, in any other room in the house. I had been shown a wardrobe with some hanging space above a shelf where, I was told, I could put my 'linen'. This misunderstanding was soon sorted out; by 'linen' I was not meant to understand sheets and pillowcases (which of course I had not brought with me) but any clothes which didn't hang up, such as underwear, and the wardrobe was intended to house all one's clothes.

The typical French country bedroom is a charming place, a fusion of the simple and the sophisticated. The wooden floor is polished and bare, except perhaps for a handsome rug. The window is likely to possess a traditional pair of tall, overlapping casements, secured with a twist-action long-bolt fastening and veiled with a simple net curtain. The bed may be narrow and not especially comfortable, but it will probably have a prettily carved head and foot.

The wardrobe will often take up a large part of the remaining space and in the corner there may be a simple handbasin with old chrome taps. This will sometimes be hidden from the rest of the room by an elegant little fabric-covered folding screen. The extreme fastidiousness of such an arrangement may seem startling at first, but it makes sense. After all, who enjoys looking at half-empty bottles and jars and half-squeezed tubes of toothpaste?

The strangest room in an old-fashioned French country house, however, is likely to be the lavatory. I once visited a house where this was a narrow, dark room with a small window at the opposite end from the door. Just below the window was an edifice

This kitchen chair and the traditional Provençal fabric covering the cushion were picked up by the owners in their local market.

which resembled a throne. A polished wooden bench filled the entire width of the room and had a broad step on which one climbed to reach the seat. This was a smooth round hole carved in the bench and covered with a lid. To flush the lavatory, you reached into a small indentation near the seat and lifted a porcelain knob which activated a deafening gush of water. Many old country houses are still more likely to rely on a cesspit rather than mains sewerage.

One of the greatest fans of French style in all its forms is the British designer Terence Conran, who once summed up his feelings with the words: 'All the best things come from France.' In the introduction to his book *Terence Conran's France* he describes the enormous impression made upon him by his first visit to the country, in 1952. 'I took in the excitement, colour and graphic abundance of the street markets, the beauty of shabby exterior decay on rural buildings, the light and texture of the countryside, and the fresh, functional design of everything from advertising typography to enamelled coffee pots ... '

His love of all things French has been infectious: during his years as a retailer with the Habitat and Conran shops in Britain, continental Europe, the USA and Japan, he has introduced a whole generation of people to the joys of owning and using well-designed French kitchenware. He popularized such objects as the cafetière and the wooden salad bowl, without which no contemporary home is complete today, but which were almost unheard of outside continental Europe before the first Habitat shop opened in May 1964 in the Fulham Road in London. Needless to say, Terence Conran has a house in the French countryside where he spends part of the year. Would that every francophile amongst us could do the same! If we could, however, there would barely be a Frenchman left in the countryside to perpetuate the magnificent charm and warmth of true French country style.

DOORS

In a French country house, the craftsmanship displayed in the design of ironwork such as door fittings is likely to be
superb; and the style and finish of the
doors themselves will give you a clue as
to what lies within...

A magnificent rim latch and lock with curlicue handle,
original to the kitchen door which it fastens in a mid-
eighteenth-century bastide *in Provence.*

This solid, matt-painted, dusty-blue plank door complete with a window hatch belongs to a farm cottage in Brittany.

An old straw boater hangs from one of two decorative hooks on the back of a blue-painted door in a house in Les Landes.

One of two solid oak front doors opening into a traditional Provençal bastide. The ironwork on the door is substantial and magnificent: knob, knocker, fingerplate and huge nails studding the lower part all illustrate the skill and artistry of local ferronniers or blacksmiths.

The doorknob on the front door (left) is a delightful illustration of the blacksmith's art. The knob is constructed from a whorl of squared iron strands, each of which has been twisted. The strands come together behind a solid blob of iron.

*Another delightful piece of ironwork, this time a bedroom door handle upstairs in
the Provençal bastide.*

A pretty brass bedroom door-bolt which, in spite of its six screws attaching it to the door, is hardly robust.

A magnificent brass bedroom window-catch. This bedroom belonged to the lady of the house, so the fittings are especially fine.

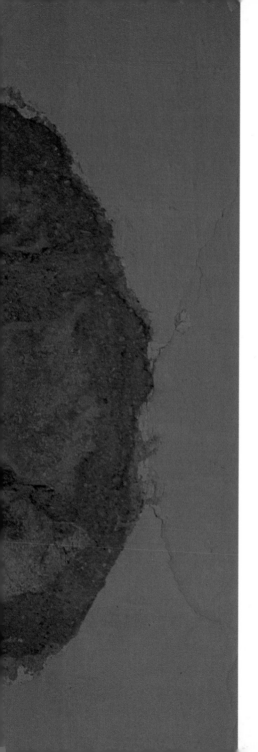

FLOORS, STAIRS & WINDOWS

France has given its name to the generous and practical, full-length opening 'French window', found the world over. No wonder windows in French country houses are so delectable, as are simple floors and staircases.

This tiny unglazed window has recently been punched through a wall to ventilate a new bathroom. It reveals the thickness of the wall, which helps keep the old mill warm in winter and cool in summer.

Old terracotta floor tiles in Provence. The lozenge shaped ones are, predictably, more unusual than the plain squares. Tiles and stone floors help to keep houses cool in the terrific heat of summer.

These ancient chestnut floorboards taper because they were cut from whole trees. This mill is still surrounded by chestnut groves of the type from which the wood, naturally impervious to beetles, has been cut for centuries to make almost everything found locally.

*This type of straight-up, rustic staircase with no banister rail is known as an
échelle de meunier, a 'miller's ladder', and in this case that was literally so, since
the stairs lead to the former granary in an old mill. The banisters visible at the top
were made from a manger found in the cattle shed on the ground floor of the house.*

A staircase constructed from stone, wood, tiles and iron, the newel (or bottom post) revealing once again the Provençal craftsman's skill with wrought iron.

Another échelle de meunier, *this time without any support on one side, making it especially precarious, even for a sober adult.*

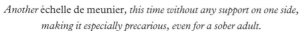

The colours used on the woodwork and exterior of Provençal houses are vivid and fresh when applied, but quickly and beautifully fade in the blazing summer sun.

These enamel jugs, with their pretty arrangement of dried grasses, stand in an original stone sink beneath a newer window in the kitchen of a centuries-old mill in south-west France.

A particularly pretty window fastening. When the handle is lifted from the catch,
the left-hand casement can be opened slightly to allow air in. The handle may then
be dropped to secure the window from swinging further open.

A blue-painted iron window catch of particularly elegant design incorporating star shapes, with a pretty brass knob.

PATTERN
& COLOUR

PATTERNED FRENCH FABRICS, SUCH AS TRA-

DITIONAL PROVENÇAL PRINTS WITH THEIR

LUSCIOUS COLOURS AND DESIGNS, ARE AMONG

THE MOST COVETED IN THE WORLD, AND THE

FRENCH USE OF PATTERN IS AMONG THE

BOLDEST.

*A handsome mid-nineteenth-century carved and
painted wooden bed was upholstered with this fabric in
the 1940s; the pattern complements the hand-blocked
wallpaper which is original to this early nineteenth-
century house.*

White tiles with a fresh blue and yellow pattern line this bathroom; the chrome towel rail is typical of this house which has one by every basin.

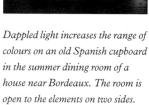

Dappled light increases the range of colours on an old Spanish cupboard in the summer dining room of a house near Bordeaux. The room is open to the elements on two sides.

Detail of the magnificent table 'carpet' on page 13

The traditional fabrics of Provence are based on Indian prints imported into France in the seventeenth century and are still produced by the company Souleiado, using modern techniques. This fabric is No. 1078-05 (Petite fleur des champs) *from* La Collection Traditionelle, *with border No. 1459-01* (La Pitchune).

Another ravishing Souleiado fabric in a mas *in the Camargue, this time No. 1402-00, called* La Pompadour, *with a magnificent wide border No. 1405-0 (*Le grand rose). *Souleiado fabrics are available outside France and there is also a catalogue (see acknowledgements on page 80).*

Wallpaper decorated with a pattern in the grand style, in the salon of a house in the Loire. The function of the chair rail is to protect the lower paper from damage by chair backs and feet.

A close-up view of a remarkable piece of craftsmanship, a huge bedcover made by the owner's grandmother in 1910. The white cotton crocheted cover has been made to a particular design which is a Provençal speciality.

KITCHENS

The contemplation, preparation and consumption of fresh food is a serious national pastime in France. The kitchen therefore tends to be the focus of the home, especially in the country, and is filled with delicious sights and smells.

A collection of enamelware, including a set of six kitchen storage jars found at a summer brocante *fair. In France, only objects that are a hundred years old or more count as antique; the rest are know as '*brocante*', roughly translatable as 'high class junk'.*

A deliciously welcoming scene in the home of writer Peter Mayle near Menerbes in the Luberon district of Provence.
The elegant shelves on the back wall are antique and were once a baker's display.

*The kitchen is the heart of the house in many French country homes such as this one, where assorted chairs,
including a rush-seated child's high chair, are gathered around a table covered with patterned cloth.*

A shallow eighteenth-century kitchen sink made from a type of granite found in north-eastern France and local to this house.

The contemplation and consumption of food are national pastimes in France, with good reason. This corner of a French kitchen is crammed with utensils and, most important, vegetables, bread and cheese.

The hatch of a charbonnière, *a sort of mobile coal bunker. This one is kept close to the range that it feeds (right) but can be wheeled away on its castors to be refilled.*

An extraordinary enamelled cast-iron range in a farmhouse in the Loire. It was made in about 1920 and is typical of the region – there were several manufacturers in St Etienne where there was a tradition of coal mining and iron foundry. Fired by solid fuel – either wood or coal – it is still in use today.

A dresser supporting fruity objects is surrounded by paintings of fruit by the owners of the house.

A beautiful nineteenth-century set of hooks in wirework hangs below an advertisement board promoting coffee. Whole shops were once boarded up when the owner died, because of France's complicated inheritance laws, so there is often plenty of charming ephemera like this to be found in provincial flea markets.

An early twentieth-century enamelled iron splashback on which to hang ladles and other kitchen utensils. The tray at the bottom catches any drips. Splashbacks were made with many different patterns and colours but were mostly of the same size and design. Next to it hangs a salt box.

A painted metal bottle-rack for drying washed bottles. These are still found in use in French country homes and were once also used in restaurants. Glass bottles were reused because they were more valuable than the local wine kept in them – a case of recycling from economic necessity.

Local olive oil is found alongside imported Italian oil and dried herbs from the garden on a windowsill in a Provençal kitchen. The flavour and scent of oil, herbs and garlic, with vegetables such as aubergines and peppers in season, is typical of the region's cookery.

LIVING
ROOMS

OUTSIDE THE KITCHEN, OTHER COUNTRY LIV-
ING ROOMS TEND TO BE BOLDLY DECORATED
OR FURNISHED, WITH MAGNIFICENT FURNI-
TURE LIKE THE TRADITIONAL ARMOIRE AND
PANETIÈRE.

A magnificent example of a panetière, *the typically
Provençal wall-hung cupboard in which bread is stored
to keep it fresh. Carvings on the front panels show
flowers, game and wheatsheaves.*

The owner of this house was studying interior design when she decorated the rooms using richly-coloured paints on all of the woodwork. She also removed many panels of infill between the timber supports, introducing light and air into a previously gloomy house.

A close-up of the armoire (seen left) showing in detail the exuberance of the carving down the middle, and the ferrures which help to protect the doors of the cupboard from being marked by fingerprints.

A splendid armoire in the dining room of a house in the Camargue. Storage cupboards such as this were often part of a bride's dowry. This has the typical three panels on each door with especially fine carving across the top and down the middle, and fine ferrures (metal strips) on the doors.

An early nineteenth-century inlaid floor in front of a contemporary fireplace in a country house near Moulins.

*This enamelled stove is in the same house as the enamelled kitchen range on
page 54 and was made around the same time, in the 1920s.*

The fireplace in the living room of a thousand-year-old mill in the Aveyron area of south-west France. Locals can still remember a time when they gathered around the fire, drinking, singing and gossiping while their grain was ground. When the owners bought the long-abandoned mill five years ago the cauldron over the fire was their only source of hot water.

The overmantel of the fireplace in a Breton farm cottage, edged with a pretty Christmassy baldaquin or canopy,
and used to store coffee bowls, soup plates, glasses, bottles and a paraffin lamp.

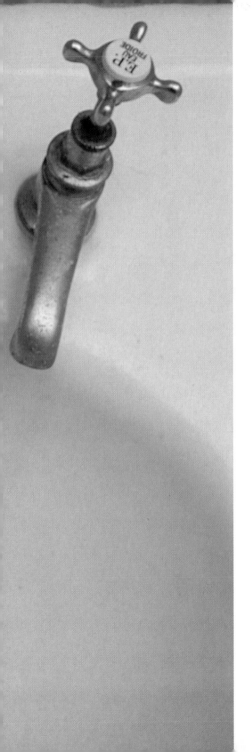

BEDROOMS
&
BATHROOMS

IN A FRENCH COUNTRY BEDROOM, THE FUR-
NISHINGS ARE LIKELY TO BE SIMPLE BUT
ELEGANT; THE BATHROOMS MAY BE UTILI-
TARIAN BUT MAGNIFICENT, WITH ANTIQUE
CHINA AND FITTINGS.

An excellent example of a solid plain white basin with
old chrome taps.

A modern brass bed covered with a bedspread made from an old piece of fabric decorated with a traditional Provençal print. This is one of the bedrooms in a Provençal bastide which the owners let on a bed-and-breakfast basis (see address in acknowledgements on page 80).

A room known as the 'Queen's Bedroom' in a mas *in the Camargue. The collection of watches and religious artefacts belonged to the owner's great-grandmother.*

Box beds in a restored farm cottage in Brittany. This bed and the one opposite are alongside each other on one wall of the cottage's only room, used for eating, cooking, sleeping and living in.

In beds like these, a huge straw mattress, perhaps 60 cm (2 ft) thick, would have been topped with a large 'duvet' filled with oat chaff, or feathers if you could afford them.

*A huge iron bath with magnificent feet and plumbing; of the four taps, the middle
two are hot and cold, the bottom operates the bath tap and the top the shower.*

A bathroom that is utilitarian but majestic in scale, with a voluptuous double basin, vast bath, handsome radiator and elegant chrome fittings. The basin was made by Porcher, a French company still in production.

Two single basins joined to make a 'double' with a neat centre panel. Sadly the original taps have been replaced with less than elegant modern mixer taps.

This charming, nineteenth-century handbasin was reclaimed from another building and installed in the recently restored ancient mill in the Aveyron.

A handsome nineteenth-century cast-iron bathroom radiator with sinuous scrolled decorations.

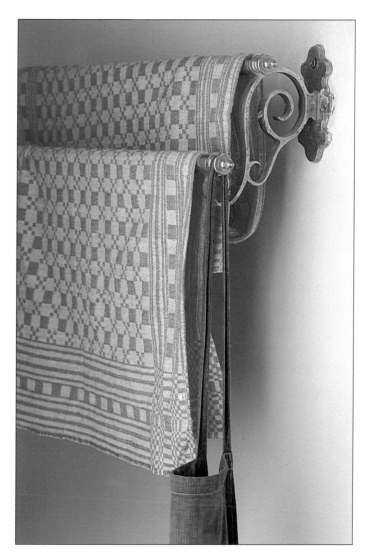

A charming chrome towel rail in the nineteenth-century house near Moulins.

ACKNOWLEDGEMENTS

DEDICATION

For my parents, in memory of the many happy times we have spent together in France.

Elizabeth Hilliard is grateful to the many people whose kindness and enthusiasm have helped her greatly with this book, but she especially thanks the following: Charles Allen; Emma Armitage; M. and Mme Pierre Rosetti Balanesco; Kate Bell; Véronique Blum; Felicity Bryan; Paul Burcher; Georgina Cardew; Conran Octopus for the extract from *Terence Conran's France*; M. and Mme d'Annunzio, whose house in Provence we photographed and who let several bedrooms for bed and breakfast at La Canal, Quartier le Grand Jardin, 83510 Lorgues, France, telephone 010 33 94 67 68 32, or in London, telephone and fax 071 602 2408; E. Jane Dickson; the *Ecomusée* at St Dégan en Brec'h, telephone 010 33 97 57 66 00; Helen Selka Farmiloe; Ros and Martin Hart, who have a brocante shop at Les Trois Arcades, Route Bleue R.N.7, 42310 La Pacaudiere, France; Annet Held; Karen Hill; Mrs David Hilliard; Alan James; Rachel King; Mme Henri Laurent; Barbara Mellor and Gavin Harding; Morten and Julia Pedersen; Souleiado: Head office: 39 rue Proudhon, 13150 Tarascon, France, telephone 010 33 90 91 08 80, fabric catalogue available in England from 171 Fulham Road, London SW3 6JW, telephone 071 589 6180, price £14.00 plus £1.50 postage and packing, and in the USA from Manuel Canovas, Inc., 979 Third Avenue, New York 10022, telephone 0101 212 752 9588; Helen Sudell; Susan Taylor.

Above all, she thanks John Miller whose beautiful photographs make this book what it is.

All photographs © John Miller except the following which are reproduced by permission of Robert Harding Syndication, copyright © IPC Magazines, courtesy of the following photographers: p.50: Peter Rauter; pp.51 & 53: N. Mackenzie; p.52 F. von der Schulenburg.